From One House to Another

to Another

Sophia Mason

ISBN-10: 0-86690-363-1
ISBN-13: 978-0-86690-363-9

Cover Design: Jack Cipolla

Published by:
American Federation of Astrologers, Inc.
6535 S. Rural Road
Tempe, AZ 85283

Printed in the United States of America

Books by Sophia Mason

Forecasting With New, Full and Quarter Moons

Basic Fundamentals of the Natal Chart

Aspects Between Signs

Understanding Planetary Placements

Lunations and Predictions

The Art of Forecasting

Delineation of Progressions

From One House To Another

You and Your Ascendant

Contents

Introduction

Fresh attention is being focused on rekindling the total use of the natal chart.

Once a thorough understanding of the houses is achieved, it is possible to predict with uncanny accuracy the affairs of others through one's own horoscope.

New astrologers often anticipate a certain transiting aspect to a natal planet, only to have it pass without any noticeable effect. Then, after a few days or weeks have passed, favorable news is heard regarding a family member or friend. If the individual were to reexamine the natal chart and correctly apply the transiting aspect to its proper house, it would be viewed with a different perspective.

There are no explanations as to why natal and transiting planets are able to reveal the affairs of others through one's own horoscope; we know only that it works with amazing accuracy.

The slower moving planets (Jupiter, Saturn, Uranus, Neptune and Pluto) are more apt to influence the affairs of others, than are the faster planets. This is due to the many aspects that the slower planets are likely to receive during their prolonged stay in one house. Using transiting Neptune in Sagittarius as an example, suppose it were transiting through your second house of money. To a certain extent Neptune will have an illusive effect on finances during its fourteen year stay in the second house. On the negative side, you must guard against possible theft, deception, confusion, and being easily led or influenced financially. On the positive side, Neptune will introduce a new and unique way of earning money. You may, for one reason or another, have to keep personal finances a secret.

To determine the illusive energy of Neptune's affect on the rest of the natal chart:

First, determine which individuals are governed by each house. Second, find the section of each chapter entitled "Your second house is their . . ." and read it from the perspective of the individual question.

For example, after reading the ninth house section, one notes that in-laws and grandchildren are listed. Your second house is their sixth house of health and work. It is possible that Neptune's stay in your second house will bring into view an illness that is difficult to diagnose or a hospital stay for either or perhaps both of these individuals.

With positive aspects to Neptune, they may decide to apply for a job with a hospital, the police department, as a security guard, or with a company that deals with gas, oils, or chemicals.

The most effective means of applying this text book is with the use of New, Full, and Quarter Moons.

For example, if the New Moon takes place in your natal tenth house, your career would be affected in some way, as would the affairs of those listed in the tenth house category. If the New Moon in your tenth house sextiles a natal or transiting planet in your twelfth house it could bring hidden (twelfth house) gains in connection with career (tenth house). However, the New Moon would also hold good news for a parent or a boss, for your twelfth house is their third house of communications.

Applying this same New Moon in the natal tenth house in a square to the ruler of your second house may indicate you will not get the raise you expected through your job. At the same time, you may hear news that your boss is having a problem with one of his/her children (your second house is your boss's fifth house of children).

An easy way to determine how transiting planets or a New or Full Moon will affect the affairs of others is to place each house on the Ascendant and count from that house to the house in which the transiting planet or New or Full Moon is positioned.

You will be astounded at how much comprehensive material and knowledge can be gained through the use of your natal chart in this manner.

First House

This is the house of the present; what is occurring now as well as beginnings and new ventures; and the individual's personal appearance, general attitude, habit, temperament, character, disposition, and health and well being. It also governs these people:

- Grandfather in a female's chart.
- Grandmother in a male's chart.
- Great grandchildren (fifth house from the ninth house).
- Marriage partner of the third sibling (brother or sister).
- Fifth child in a male's chart.
- Brothers and sisters of friends (third house from the eleventh house).
- Friends of one's brother or sister (eleventh house from the third house).
- Former marriage partner of the first mate.
- Mate's business partner.
- Mate's or business partner's third sibling.
- Nieces and nephews (the children of the individual's brother or sister-in-law).
- Marriage and business partners of nieces and nephews (nieces and nephews are the children of one's brother or sister).
- Fourth mate or business partner.

Look to the first house for the above mentioned people when dealing with the affairs of one of them. Use the native's first house as the other's first house and read the remainder of the chart accordingly (native's second house is the other's second house, etc.). For each house note all natal and transiting planets, aspects made to them and the ruler of each house. The effects, in many cases, are experienced by the people listed above.

Native's Second House Is Another's Second House

The second house governs personal finances, moveable possessions, negotiable assets, profit and loss, personal wealth and how money is spent and saved.

Native's Third House Is Another's Third House

The third house governs all forms of communication; letters, phone calls, telegrams, books, documents and contracts; the individual's mental attributes, and primary and secondary education; short trips and all forms of transportation such as busses, automobiles, bicycles, and motorcycles; accidents and minor changes; brothers, sisters, and neighbors.

Native's Fourth House Is Another's Fourth House

The fourth house governs the home, real estate, and property; emotional security and home environment; parents, family members, and individuals who reside in the native's home from time to time; older people; the grave and the affairs surrounding the latter part of life.

Native's Fifth House Is Another's Fifth House

The fifth house governs children in general, offspring, love relationships, courtship, pleasure and personal creativity; all places of amusement, theaters, entertainment, parties, schools, sporting events and participation in games and sports; gambling, speculation and investments.

2

Native's Sixth House Is Another's Sixth House

The sixth house governs health and well being; foods for maintaining individual health (vitamins and health foods); the food industry and those connected with it in selling, processing, or restaurant work; working conditions, aunts and uncles, co-workers and household appliance repairmen; inferiors, farmers, small pets and tenants; the armed forces, police, Red Cross, Peace Corps and other such volunteer organizations; clothing in general and individuals who deal with it such as dry cleaners, seamstress and tailors.

Native's Seventh House Is Another's Seventh House

The seventh house governs dealings with the general public, open enemies, litigation, contracts, physicians, attorneys, counselors, and all things of beauty; marriage and business partners, live-in relationships and sweethearts; and nieces, nephews and grandparents.

Native's Eighth House Is Another's Eighth House

The eighth house governs affairs concerned with money belonging to others; partner's earnings, legacies, wills, debts to stores, loans and alimony; income and property taxes; changes, sexuality, surgery and conditions surrounding the manner of death; nightmares, unusual dreams and compelling forces.

Native's Ninth House Is Another's Ninth House

The ninth house governs public opinion, philosophy, publishing, advertising, prophetic dreams and visions; religious affiliations, long trips, legal matters, newspapers and other published material; news from a distance; college and adult education classes; patronage of individuals of wealth and influence; people of different colors, races or cultural backgrounds.

3

Native's Tenth House Is Another's Tenth House

The tenth house governs credit rating, reputation, rank in life, scandal, career, trade and profession; those with authority over the individual, the boss, and anyone representing influence and power; a parent or an older, mature or serious kind of person; past conditions; and sometimes the culmination of a long standing problem.

Native's Eleventh House Is Another's Eleventh House

The eleventh house governs affiliations with clubs and organizations, and group activities; friends, acquaintances and individual aspirations; stepchildren, daughters-in-law and sons-in-law.

Native's Twelfth House Is Another's Twelfth House

The twelfth house governs hospitals, charitable institutions, and all places of confinement such as jails and prisons; secret enemies, secret sorrows, hidden relationships and clandestine affairs; detective, investigative or behind the scenes activities; suicides, drugs, alcohol, limitations and restrictions; unforeseen forces, incidents and circumstances; secret, weird or unusual fears; aunts and uncles; and self-imposed isolation to work in solitude on a difficult project or undertake studies of metaphysical, healing or occult subjects.

Second House

The second house governs personal finances, moveable possessions, negotiable assets, profit and loss, personal wealth and how money is spent and saved. It also governs these people:

- Step-brothers and step-sisters (fifth house from the tenth house).
- Father's second sibling in a male's chart.
- Mother's second sibling in a female's chart.
- Boyfriends's father in a female's chart (this is a fifth house lover).
- Girlfriend's mother in a male's chart (this is a fifth house lover).
- Boss of the first child in a male's chart.
- Friend of the family.
- First child of a boss or superior.
- Romantic attachment of a boss or superior.
- Romantic attachment of a boss or superior.
- Father of a female friend.
- Mother of a male friend.

Look to the second house for the above mentioned people when dealing with the affairs of one of them. Use the native's second house as the other's first and read the remainder of the chart accordingly (native's third house is the other's second house, etc.). For each house note all natal and transiting planets, aspects made to them and the ruler of each house. The effects, in many cases, are experienced by the people listed above. It may be easier to view affairs of others if you place them in a first house position, and then read the remainder of the houses as though they were the native's own chart.

Native's Third House Is Another's Second House
The second house governs personal finances, moveable possessions, negotiable assets, profit and loss, personal wealth, and how money is spent or saved.

Native's Fourth House Is Another's Third House
The fourth house governs all forms of communication; letters, phone calls, telegrams, books, documents and contracts; the individual's mental attributes, and primary and secondary education; short trips and all forms of transportation such as busses, automobiles, bicycles and motorcycles; accidents and minor changes; and brothers, sisters and neighbors.

The fourth house (third house from the second house) governs contracts, documents, letters and short trips connected with money, moveable possessions and personal finances.

Native's Fifth House Is Another's Fourth House
The fourth house governs the home, real estate and property; emotional security and home environment; parents, family members and individuals who reside in the individual's home from time to time; older people; the grave and affairs surrounding the latter part of life.

The fifth house (second house from the fourth house) deals with financial gain or loss through the sale or purchase of real estate and through rental property.

Native's Sixth House Is Another's Fifth House

The fifth house governs children in general, offspring, love relationships, courtship, pleasure and personal creativity; all places of amusement, theaters, entertainment, parties, schools, sporting events and participation in games and sports; gambling, speculation and investments and financial gain or loss through gambling, lottery and games of chance (sixth house is the second house from the fifth house).

Native's Seventh House Is Another's Sixth House

The sixth house governs health and well being; foods for maintaining health (vitamins and health foods); the food industry and those connected with it in selling, processing or restaurant work; working conditions, co-workers and household appliance repairmen; inferiors, farmers, small pets and tenants; the armed forces, police, Red Cross, Peace Corps and other such volunteer organizations; clothing in general and individuals who deal with it such as dry cleaners, seamstresses and tailors; and aunts and uncles.

Native's Eighth House Is Another's Seventh House

The seventh house governs dealings with the general public, open enemies, litigation, contracts, physicians, attorneys, counselors, and all things of beauty; marriage and business partners, live-in relationships and sweethearts; and nieces, nephews and grandparents.

Native's Ninth House Is Another's Eighth House

The eighth house governs affairs concerned with money belonging to others; the partner's earnings, legacies, wills, debts to stores, loans, and alimony; income and property taxes; sexuality, changes, surgery and conditions surrounding the manner of death; nightmares, unusual dreams and compelling forces.

Native's Tenth House Is Another's Ninth House

The ninth house governs public opinion, philosophy, publishing, advertising, prophetic dreams and visions; religious affiliations, long trips, legal matters, newspapers and other published material; news from a distance; higher education; the patronage of individuals of wealth and influence, and those of different colors, races and backgrounds.

The tenth house governs (ninth house from the second house) legal involvement with the native's personal finances or moveable possessions. Higher education, publications or long distance travel may in some way help or hinder personal finances.

Native's Eleventh House Is Another's Tenth House

The tenth house governs credit rating, reputation, rank in life, scandal, career, trade and profession; those with authority over the native, a boss or anyone representing influence and power; a parent or an older, mature or serious person; past conditions; and sometimes the culmination of a long standing situation.

Native's Twelfth House Is Another's Eleventh House

The eleventh house governs affiliations with clubs and organizations, and group activities; friends, acquaintances and individual aspirations; daughters-in-law, sons-in-law and step-children.

Native's First House Is Another's Twelfth House

The twelfth house governs hospitals, charitable institutions and all places of confinement such as jails and prisons; secret enemies, secret sorrows, hidden relationships and clandestine affairs; detective, investigative or behind the scenes activities; suicides, drugs, alcohol, limitations and restrictions. unforeseen forces, incidents and circumstances; secret, weird or unusual fears; and aunts and uncles.

Third House

The third house governs individual mental attributes, and primary and secondary education; short trips, all forms of communication, letters, phone calls, documents and contracts; all forms of transportation such as cars, busses, bicycles and motorcycles; accidents and minor changes. The third house also governs these people:

- First sibling (brother or sister).
- Neighbors.
- Neighborhood merchants.
- Children of friends (fifth house from the eleventh house).
- Children of one's daughter or son-in-law through a previous marriage (fifth house from the eleventh house).
- Children of friends (fifth house from the eleventh house).
- Marriage partner of the native's ninth house brother-in-law or sister-in-law (the mate's first sibling).
- Marriage partner of the third child in a male's chart.
- Friends of the native's children (eleventh house from the fifth house).
- Parent of a co-worker (tenth house from the sixth house).
- First grandchild's marriage or business partner.

Look to the third house for the above mentioned people when dealing with the affairs of one of them. Use the native's third house as the other's first and read the remainder of the chart accordingly (native's fourth house is the other's second house, etc.). For example, if the native's oldest sister wishes to sell her house, look to the native's sixth house, which is the fourth house from the native's third house. Note all natal and transiting planets, aspects made to them and the ruler of each house. The effects, in many cases, are experienced by the people listed above.

Native's Fourth House Is Another's Second House

The second house governs personal finances, moveable possessions, negotiable assets, profit and loss, personal wealth and how money is spent and saved.

The fourth house (second house from the third house) governs money that is gained or lost through speaking engagements, teaching, written material, books, salesmanship, automobiles, accidents and short travels.

Native's Fifth House Is Another's Third House

The third house governs all forms of communication; letters, phone calls, telegrams, books, documents and contracts; the individual's mental attributes, and primary and secondary education; short trips and all forms of transportation such as busses, automobiles, bicycles, and motorcycles; accidents and minor changes; brothers, sisters and neighbors.

The fifth house (third house from the third house) governs documents, communication and the signing of contracts that deal with salesmanship, book printing, lecturing and teaching.

Native's Sixth House Is Another's Fourth House

The fourth house governs the home, real estate, and property; emotional security and home environment; parents, family members, and individuals who reside in the individual's home from time to time; older people; the grave and the affairs surrounding the latter part of life. The sixth house also governs the end of the matter regarding third house documents, news, short trips and communications.

Native's Seventh House Is Another's Fifth House

The fifth house governs children in general, offspring, love relationships, courtship, pleasure and personal creativity; all places of amusement, theaters, entertainment, parties, schools, sporting events and participation in games and sports; and gambling, speculation and investments.

Native's Eighth House Is Another's Sixth House

The sixth house governs health and well being; foods for maintaining health (vitamins and health foods); the food industry and those connected with it as in selling, processing and restaurant work; working conditions, co-workers and household appliance repairmen; inferiors, farms, small pets and tenants; the armed forces, police, Red Cross, Peace Corps and other such volunteer organizations; clothing in general and individuals who deal with it such as dry cleaners, seamstress and tailors; and aunts and uncles.

Native's Ninth House Is Another's Seventh House

The seventh house governs dealings with the general public, open enemies, litigation, contracts, physicians, attorneys, counselors, and all things of beauty; marriage and business partners, live-in relationships and sweethearts; and nieces, nephews and grandparents.

Native's Tenth House Is Another's Eighth House

The eighth house governs affairs concerned with money belonging to others; the partner's earnings, legacies, wills, debts to stores, loans and alimony; income and property taxes; sexuality, change, surgery, conditions surrounding the manner of death; nightmares, unusual dreams and compelling forces.

Native's Eleventh House Is Another's Ninth House

The ninth house governs public opinion, philosophy, publishing, advertising, prophetic dreams and visions; religious affiliations, long trips, legal matters; published material; news from a distance; higher education; the patronage of individuals of wealth and influence; people of different colors, races and backgrounds. The eleventh house (ninth house from the third house) governs lawsuits through verbal statements, contracts and written agreements; lawsuits resulting from or through accidents; long distance communication from brothers or sisters.

Native's Twelfth House Is Another's Tenth House

The tenth house governs credit rating, reputation, rank in life, scandal, career, trade and profession; those with authority over the individual, the boss, parent and anyone representing influence and power; past conditions; and sometimes the culmination of a long standing situation.

The twelfth house (tenth house from the third house) governs publicity, scandal or loss of reputation through spoken or written words, accidents or short trips.

Native's First House Is Another's Eleventh House

The eleventh house governs affiliations with clubs and organizations, and group activities; friends, acquaintances, the individual's aspirations; and daughters-in-law, sons-in-law and step-children. The first house (eleventh house from the third house) governs friendships made through teaching positions, short trips, and various means of communication such as letters, telephone calls and pen pals.

Native's Second House Is Another's Twelfth House

The twelfth house governs hospitals, charitable institutions, and all places of confinement such as jails and prisons; secret enemies, secret sorrows, hidden relationships and clandestine affairs; detective, investigative and behind the scenes activities; suicides, drugs, alcohol, limitations and restrictions; unforeseen forces, incidents and circumstances; secret, weird or unusual fears; and aunts and uncles. The second house (twelfth house from the third house) governs deception, secrecy and confusion concerning documents, contracts, accidents and short trips.

Fourth House

The fourth house governs the home, real estate, property and land developments; emotional security and home environment; parents, family members and individuals who reside in the native's home at one time or another; older people; and the grave, the end of life and the affairs surrounding the latter part of life. Natives with more than one planet in the fourth house often develop an interest in working with real estate, managing hotels or apartment buildings, and working in areas involving restaurants, catering, bakeries, foods and farming. The fourth house also governs these people:

Parents, parents-in-law and step-parents; the male parent in a female's chart and the female parent in a male's chart.

- Co-worker of a friend (sixth house from the eleventh house).
- First child in a female's chart.
- Boss' marriage partner.
- Father's third sibling in a male's chart.
- Mother's third sibling in a female's chart.
- Father's first niece or nephew in a male's chart (child of the father's first sibling).
- Mother's first niece or nephew in a female's chart; child of the father's first sibling (fifth house from the twelfth house

of aunts and uncles).
- Marriage partner of the fourth child in a female's chart.
- Marriage partner's boss.

Look to the fourth house for the above mentioned people when dealing with the affairs of one of them. Use the native's fourth house as the other's first house and read the remainder of the chart accordingly (native's fifth house is the other's second house, etc.). For each house, note all natal and transiting planets, aspects made to them and the ruler of each house. The effects, in many cases, are experienced by the people listed above.

Native's Fifth House Is Another's Second House
The second house governs personal finances, moveable possessions, negotiable assets, profit and loss, personal wealth and how money is spent and saved. The fifth house (second house from the fourth house) governs financial gain or loss through the selling of land, property and real estate, or through rental property.

Native's Sixth House Is Another's Third House
The third house governs all forms of communication; letters, phone calls, telegrams, books, documents and contracts; the individual's mental attributes, and primary and secondary education; short trips and all forms of transportation such as busses, automobiles, bicycles and motorcycles; accidents and minor changes; and brothers, sisters and neighbors.

The sixth house (third house from the fourth house) governs all written documents, contracts, news and short trips that are connected with land deals, real estate, and buying and selling property governed by this house.

Native's Seventh House Is Another's Fourth House

The fourth house governs the home, real estate and property; emotional security and home environment; parents, family members and individuals who reside in the individual's home from time to time; older people; and the grave and the affairs surrounding the latter part of life.

The seventh house is the end of the matter for fourth house property and real estate dealings.

Native's Eighth House Is Another's Fifth House

The fifth house governs children in general, offspring, love relationships, courtship, pleasure and personal creativity; all places of amusement, theaters, entertainment, parties, schools, sporting events and participation in games and sports; and gambling, speculation and investments.

Native's Ninth House Is Another's Sixth House

The sixth house governs health and well being; food for maintaining health (vitamins and health foods); the food industry and those connected with it in selling, processing and restaurant work; working conditions, co-workers and household appliance repairmen; inferiors, farmers, small pets and tenants; armed forces, police, Red Cross, Peace Corps and other such volunteer organizations; clothing in general, dry cleaners, seamstresses, and tailors; and aunts and uncles.

The ninth house (sixth house from the fourth house) governs the maintenance and sanitary condition of one's home, land or property.

Native's Tenth House Is Another's Seventh House

The seventh house governs dealings with the general public, open enemies, litigation, contracts, physicians, attorneys, coun-

selors, and all things of beauty; the marriage and business partners, live-in relationships and sweethearts; and nieces, nephews and grandparents.

The tenth house is the end of the matter for divorce, marriage and business partnerships, and contracts.

Native's Eleventh House Is Another's Eighth House
The eighth house governs money belonging to others; the partner's earnings, legacies, wills, debts to stores, loans and alimony; income and property taxes; sexuality, changes, surgery and conditions surrounding the manner of death; nightmares, unusual dreams and compelling forces.

The eleventh house (eighth house from the fourth house) governs change regarding land, property and real estate.

Native's Twelfth House Is Another's Ninth House
The ninth house governs public opinion, philosophy, publishing, advertising, prophetic dreams and visions; religious affiliations, long trips, legal matters, newspapers and other published material; news from a distance; higher education; the patronage of individuals of wealth and influence; and people of different colors, races or backgrounds.

The twelfth house (ninth house from the fourth house) governs legal matters in connection with property, land and real estate.

Native's First House Is Another's Tenth House
The tenth house governs credit rating, reputation, rank in life, scandal, careers, trades and professions; those with authority over the individual, the boss, parent, and anyone representing influence and power; past conditions; sometimes the culmination of a long standing situation.

Native's Second House Is Another's Eleventh House

The eleventh house governs affiliations with clubs and organizations, and group activities; friends, acquaintances, the individual's aspirations; and daughters-in-law, sons-in-law and step-children.

The second house (fourth house from the third house) governs clubs and organizations that may be affiliated with homes and property, or operated from the home.

Native's Third House Is Another's Twelfth House

The twelfth house governs hospitals, charitable institutions and all places of confinement such as jails and prisons; secret enemies, secret sorrows, hidden relationships and clandestine affairs; detective, investigative or behind the scenes activities; suicides, drugs, alcohol, limitations and restrictions; unforeseen forces, incidents and circumstances; secret, weird and unusual fears; and aunts and uncles.

The third house (twelfth house from the fourth house) governs hidden gains or losses, secrets, hidden factors and deception from or through land, property and real estate in addition to secret fears regarding one's emotional security, old age and the latter part of life.

Fifth House

The fifth house governs all places of amusement, theaters, schools, parties, entertainment, sporting events and participation in games and sports; gambling, speculation and investments; love relationships, children in general, offspring, courtship and pleasure; and personal creativity. It also governs these people:

- Children in general.
- First child in a male's chart.
- Marriage partner of a friend (seventh house from the eleventh house).
- Marriage or business partner of a step-child (seventh house from the eleventh house).
- Marriage or business partner of the fourth child in a male's chart.
- Second sibling (brother or sister).
- Lover or romantic attachment.
- Friend of the husband or wife (eleventh house from the seventh house).
- Domestic pet regarded as a child.
- Entertainer.

Look to the fifth house for the above mentioned people when dealing with the affairs of one of them. Use the native's fifth house as the other's first house and read the remainder of the chart accordingly (native's sixth house is the other's second house, etc.). For each house note all natal and transiting planets, aspects made to them and the ruler of each house. The effects, in many cases, will be experienced by the people listed above.

Native's Sixth House Is Another's Second House

The second house governs personal finances, moveable possessions, negotiable assets, profit and loss, personal wealth and how money is spent and saved.

The sixth house (second house from the fifth house) governs financial gain and loss from sports, games of chance, lotteries, gambling and all forms of pleasure, entertainment and speculation.

Native's Seventh House Is Another's Third House

The third house governs all forms of communication; letters, phone calls, telegrams, books, documents and contracts; the individual's mental attributes, and primary and secondary education; short trips and all forms of transportation such as busses, automobiles, bicycles, and motorcycles; accidents and minor changes; brothers, sisters and neighbors.

The seventh house (third house from the fifth house) governs letters or other communication from the school system or regarding children; short field trips planned by the school system; invitations to social functions; and accidents that occur at schools and sporting events.

Native's Eighth House Is Another's Fourth House

The fourth house governs the home, real estate and property; emotional security and home environment; parents, family members and individuals who reside in the individual's home from time to time; older people; the grave and affairs surrounding the latter part of life. The eighth house (fourth house from the fifth house) governs the final outcome of romantic relationships and affairs of children.

Native's Ninth House Is Another's Fifth House
The fifth house governs children in general, offspring, love relationships, courtship, pleasure and personal creativity; all places of amusement, theaters, entertainment, parties, schools, sporting events and participation in games and sports; and gambling, speculation and investments.

The ninth house (fifth house from the fifth house) governs travel for pleasurable pursuits, vacation, gambling purposes and to visit children living in distant places.

Native's Tenth House Is Another's Sixth House
The sixth house governs affairs concerned with health and well being; foods for maintaining health (vitamins and health foods); the food industry and those connected with it in selling, processing and restaurant work; working conditions, co-workers and household appliance repairmen; inferiors, farmers, small pets and tenants; the armed forces, police, Red Cross, Peace Corps and other such volunteer organizations; clothing in general and individuals who deal with it such as dry cleaners, seamstresses and tailors; and aunts and uncles.

The tenth house (sixth house from the fifth house) governs health and working conditions of one's romantic partner.

Native's Eleventh House Is Another's Seventh House
The seventh house governs dealings with the general public, open enemies, litigations, contracts, physicians, attorneys, counselors, and all things of beauty; marriage and business part-

ners, live in relationships and sweethearts; nieces, nephews and grandparents.

The eleventh house (seventh house from the fifth house) governs open enemies of the fifth house children or one's romantic interest.

Native's Twelfth House Is Another's Eighth House
The eighth house governs affairs concerned with money belonging to others; the partner's earnings, legacies, wills, debts to stores, loans and alimony; income and property taxes; sexuality, changes, surgery and conditions surrounding the manner of death; nightmares, unusual dreams and compelling forces.

The twelfth house (eighth house from the fifth house) governs sexual response and attitude in connection with love affairs.

Native's First House Is Another's Ninth House
The ninth house governs public opinion, philosophy, publishing, advertising, prophetic dreams and visions; religious affiliations, long trips, legal matters, newspapers and other published material; news from a distance; higher education; the patronage of individuals of wealth and influence; and those of different colors, races and backgrounds.

The first house (ninth house from the fifth house) governs long distance travel undertaken for entertainment and for the enjoyment of watching a certain entertainer perform; travel undertaken by school children in connection with educational programs (field trips); long distance travel for the purpose of gambling (trip to Las Vegas); legal action or lawsuits in connection with a child or children (not necessarily one's own); legal action taken against the school system, places of entertainment, nightclubs, theaters, stadiums and sporting events.

Native's Second House Is Another's Tenth House

The tenth house governs credit rating, reputation, rank in life, scandal, career, trade and profession; those with authority over the individual, the boss, parent, and anyone representing influence and power; past conditions; and sometimes the culmination of a long standing situation.

The second house (tenth house from the fifth house) governs the reputation, publicity and scandal concerning love affairs, children, pleasure and gambling debts.

Native's Third House Is Another's Eleventh House

The eleventh house governs affiliations with clubs and organizations and group activities; friends, acquaintances and individual aspirations; daughters-in-law, sons-in-law and step-children.

The third house (eleventh house from the fifth house) governs clubs and organizations involving the school system and school children (local PTA); clubs and organizations connected with the entertainment field, movie stars and famous singers (fan clubs); how well the individual relates to friends of his children and romantic attachments, and friends made through places of pleasure and entertainment.

Native's Fourth House Is Another's Twelfth House

The twelfth house governs hospitals, charitable institutions and all places of confinement such as jails and prisons; secret enemies, secret sorrows, hidden relationships and clandestine affairs; detective, investigative and behind the scenes activities; suicides, drugs, alcohol, limitations and restrictions; unforeseen forces, incidents and circumstances; secret, weird and unusual fears; and aunts and uncles.

The fourth house (twelfth house from the fifth house) governs secrets, sorrows and hidden losses or gains from or through romance, gambling, speculation and affairs of children.

Sixth House

The sixth house governs affairs concerned with illnesses, working conditions, co-workers, servicemen, repairmen (plumbers, electricians, household appliance repairmen), inferiors, farmers, small pets, tenants, foods for maintaining the health (vitamins and health foods), the armed forces, police, Red Cross, Peace Corps and other such volunteer organizations; clothing in general and individuals who deal with it such as dry cleaners, seamstresses, and tailors; restaurants where food is sold and prepared and those who work and deal in such commodities. It also governs these people:

- Aunts and uncles on the father's side in a female's chart.
- Aunts and uncles on the mother's side in a male's chart.
- Co-workers and employees.
- Tenants.
- Second child in a female's chart.
- Neighbor's parent (fourth house from the third house).
- The husband or wife of one's secret lover (seventh house from the twelfth house).

Look to the sixth house for the above mentioned people when dealing with the affairs of one of them. Use the native's sixth house as the other's first and read the remainder of the chart accordingly (native's seventh house is the other's second house). For example, if an aunt or uncle enters the hospital, look to the native's fifth house since it is the twelfth house (hospital confinement) from the sixth.

For each house note all natal and transiting planets, aspects made to them and the ruler of each house. The effects, in many cases, are experienced by the people listed above.

Native's Seventh House Is Another's Second House
The second house governs personal finances, moveable possessions, negotiable assets, profit and loss, personal wealth and how money is spent or saved.

The seventh house (second house from the sixth house) governs financial gains or losses through labor unions and working conditions; money spent on small pets; money spent on health care, hygiene, health foods, vitamins and special clothing such as uniforms or safety shoes.

Native's Eighth House Is Another's Third House
The third house governs all forms of communication; letters, phone calls, telegrams, books, documents and contracts; the individual's mental attributes, and primary and secondary education; short trips and all forms of transportation such as busses, automobiles, bicycles and motorcycles; accidents and minor changes; and brothers, sisters and neighbors.

The eighth house (third house from the sixth house) governs news, documents, letters and communication regarding work and health.

Native's Ninth House Is Another's Fourth House
The fourth house governs the home, real estate and property; emotional security and home environment; parents, family members, and individuals who reside in the individual's home

from time to time; older people; the grave and the affairs surrounding the latter part of life.

The ninth house (fourth house from the sixth house) reveals the final outcome of illnesses, health conditions and job positions. The ninth house also serves as the home base for those serving with the Peace Corps or armed forces and indicates the general condition of living quarters such as the barracks and camp sites which these people would call home.

Native's Tenth House Is Another's Fifth House

The fifth house governs children in general, offspring, one's love relationship, courtship, pleasure and personal creativity; all places of amusement, theaters, entertainment, parties, schools, sporting events and participation in games and sports; and gambling, speculation and investments.

The tenth house (fifth house from the sixth house) governs litters, puppies and kittens born to the individual's domestic pet.

Native's Eleventh House Is Another's Sixth House

The sixth house governs health and well being; foods for maintaining health (vitamins and health foods); the food industry and those connected with it in selling, processing or restaurant work; working conditions, co-workers and household appliance repairmen; inferiors, farmers, small pets and tenants; the armed forces, police, Red Cross, Peace Corps and other such volunteer organizations; clothing in general and individuals who deal with it such as dry cleaners, seamstresses and tailors; and aunts and uncles.

The eleventh house (sixth house from the sixth house) governs health, illness, working conditions and the type of work done while serving in the armed forces.

Native's Twelfth House Is Another's Seventh House

The seventh house governs dealings with the general public, open enemies, litigation, contracts, physicians, attorneys, counselors and all things of beauty; marriage and business partners, live-in relationships and sweethearts; and nieces, nephews and grandparents.

The twelfth house (seventh house from the sixth house) governs binding contracts that are signed concerning a job or with employment agencies while seeking a position; partnerships formed through the workplace or with a co-worker.

Native's First House Is Another's Eighth House

The eighth house governs money belonging to others; the partner's earnings, legacies, wills, debts to stores, loans and alimony; income and property taxes; sexuality, changes, surgery and conditions surrounding the manner of death; and nightmares, unusual dreams and compelling forces.

The first house (eighth house from the sixth house) governs changes within or the elimination of the individual's job due to new equipment or techniques introduced in the workplace; death and surgery of aunts and uncles, small pets and animals; debts occurring as a result of illnesses; the general trend or change of condition of an illness, either for better or worse depending upon the planet in the first house and aspects thereto.

Native's Second House Is Another's Ninth House

The ninth house governs public opinion, philosophy, publishing, advertising, prophetic dreams and visions; religious affiliations, long trips, legal matters, newspapers and other published material; news from a distance; higher education; the patronage of individuals of wealth and influence; and those of different colors, races or backgrounds.

The second house (ninth house from the sixth house) governs legal action and lawsuits occurring as a result of injuries, bites or mental anguish resulting from the actions of small pets; long distance travel undertaken to possibly improve the state of health, legal action or lawsuits occurring as a result of injury or accident through the workplace or an employee.

Native's Third House Is Another's Tenth House
The tenth house governs credit rating, reputation, rank in life, scandal, career, trade and profession; those with authority over the individual, the boss, parent and anyone representing influence and power; past conditions; and sometimes the culmination of a long standing situation.

Because the sixth house governs volunteer work, the third house (tenth house from the sixth house) may indicate public recognition received through work performed for the armed forces or volunteer organizations.

Native's Fourth House Is Another's Eleventh House
The eleventh house governs affiliations with clubs and organizations, and group activities; friends, acquaintances and individual aspirations; and daughters-in-law, sons-in-law and step-children.

The fourth house (eleventh house from the sixth house) governs friends made through the armed forces, Red Cross, Peace Corps and other such volunteer organizations; and clubs and organizations joined to improve the health (Weight Watchers, health spa).

Native's Fifth House Is Another's Twelfth House
The twelfth house governs hospitals, charitable institutions and all places of confinement such as jails and prisons; secret

enemies, secret sorrows, hidden relationships and clandestine affairs; detective, investigative and behind the scenes activities; suicides, drugs, alcohol, limitations and restrictions; unforeseen forces, incidents and circumstances; secret, weird and unusual fears; and aunts and uncles; hidden factors concerning working conditions and labor unions.

Seventh House

The seventh house deals with companionship, love of justice, peace and harmony, the mate, partnerships, general public, open enemies, litigation, contracts, physicians, attorneys, counselors, sweethearts and all things of beauty; finer wearing apparel, jewelry, art, sociability, interior decorating, furriers, beauticians, cosmeticians, florists and all matters connected with marriage or divorce. The seventh house also governs these people:

- First marriage or business partner.
- Third sibling (brother or sister).
- Nieces and nephews (fifth house from the third house).
- Marriage or business partners of nieces and nephews (children of the brother or sister-in-law).
- Second child in a male's chart.
- Marriage or business partner of the fifth child in a male's chart.
- Grandfather in a male's chart.
- Grandmother in a female's chart.
- Attorney.
- Astrologer.
- Open enemies.
- Individuals who provide services, such as a certified public accountant or marriage and school counselors.

Look to the seventh house for the above mentioned people when dealing with their affairs. Use the native's seventh house as the other's first house and read the remainder of the chart accordingly (native's eighth house is the other's second house, etc.). For each house note all natal and transiting planets, aspects made to them and the ruler of each house. The effects, in many cases, are experienced by the people listed above.

Native's Eighth House Is Another's Second House
The second house governs personal finances, moveable possessions, negotiable assets, profit and loss, personal wealth and how money is spent and saved.

The eighth house (third house from the sixth house) governs news and bulletins concerning work related duties or the employment scene.

Native's Ninth House Is Another's Third House
The third house governs all forms of communication; letters, phone calls, telegrams, books, documents and contracts; individual mental attributes, and primary and secondary education; short trips and all forms of transportation such as busses, automobiles, bicycles and motorcycles; accidents and minor changes; and brothers, sisters and neighbors.

The ninth house (third house from the seventh house) governs decisions by judges and juries concerning litigation.

Native's Tenth House Is Another's Fourth House
The fourth house governs the home, real estate and property; emotional security and home environment; parents, family members and individuals who reside in the native's home from time to time; older people; the grave and the affairs surrounding the latter part of life.

The tenth house (fourth house from the seventh house) offers a clue to the final outcome or end of the matter concerning divorce, marriage, partnerships, contracts and litigation.

Native's Eleventh House Is Another's Fifth House

The fifth house governs children in general, offspring, love relationships, courtship, pleasure and personal creativity; all places of amusement, theaters, entertainment, parties, schools, sporting events and participation in games and sports; and gambling, speculation and investments.

The eleventh house (sixth house from the sixth house) governs illnesses resulting from the working environment, such as excessive amounts of dust or asbestos in the air, or illness through odors from things such as fumes from paints and gases.

Native's Twelfth House Is Another's Sixth House

The sixth house governs health and well being; foods for maintaining health (vitamins and health foods); the food industry and those connected with it in selling, processing and restaurant work, working conditions, co-workers and household appliance repairmen; inferiors, farmers, small pets and tenants; the armed forces, police, Red Cross, Peace Corps and other such volunteer organizations; clothing in general and individuals who deal with it such as dry cleaners, seamstresses and tailors; and aunts and uncles.

Native's First House Is Another's Seventh House

The seventh house governs dealings with the general public, open enemies, litigation, contracts, physicians, attorneys, counselors and all things of beauty; marriage and business partners, live-in relationships and sweethearts; and nieces, nephews and grandparents.

Native's Second House Is Another's Eighth House

The second house governs money belonging to others; the partner's earnings, legacies, wills, debts to stores, loans and alimony; income and property taxes; sexuality, changes, surgery and conditions surrounding the manner of death; and nightmares, unusual dreams and compelling forces.

Native's Third House Is Another's Ninth House

The ninth house governs public opinion, philosophy, publishing, advertising, prophetic dreams and visions; religious affiliations, long trips, legal matters, newspapers and other published material; news from a distance; higher education; the patronage of individuals of wealth and influence; and those of different colors, races and backgrounds.

The third house (ninth house from the seventh house) governs the religious views and intellectual differences that may cause disharmony in marriage; lawsuits involving the individual's physician or attorney; and legal documents signed in connection with marriage or business partnerships and divorce.

Native's Fourth House Is Another's Tenth House

The tenth house governs credit rating, reputation, rank in life, scandal, career, trade and profession. Those in authority over the individual, the boss, parent and anyone representing influence and power; past conditions; and sometimes the culmination of a long standing situation.

The fourth house (tenth house from the seventh house) governs public notice, reputation and scandal surrounding the affairs of a divorce or litigation.

Native's Fifth House Is Another's Eleventh House

The eleventh house governs affiliations with clubs and organizations, and group activities; friends, acquaintances and individual aspirations; and daughters-in-law, sons-in-law and step-children.

The fifth house (the eleventh house from the seventh) governs friends that are met and made through social functions and through one's partner.

Native's Sixth House Is Another's Twelfth House

The twelfth house governs hospitals, charitable institutions and all places of confinement such as jails and prisons; secret enemies, secret sorrows, hidden relationships and clandestine affairs; detective, investigative and behind the scenes activities; suicides, drugs, alcohol, limitations and restrictions; unforeseen forces, incidents and circumstances; secret, weird and unusual fears; and aunts and uncles.

The fifth house (twelfth house from the seventh house) governs losses and limitations through marriage and business partners.

Eighth House

The eighth house deals with masses of people, group cooperation and activities; ESP, nightmares, unusual dreams, spirituality, the occult and seances; underhanded tactics, dictators, gangsters, compelling forces and inversion; affairs concerned with money belonging to others; partner's money, legacies, wills, credit card debt, loans and mortgage payments; alimony, income and property taxes, retirement funds and social security; property in escrow; changes in attitude, situation and conditions; and sexuality, surgery, surgeons and conditions surrounding an individual's death. The eighth house also governs these people:

- Step-brothers and step-sisters on the step-father's side in a female's chart and the step-mother's side in a male's chart.
- Third child in a female's chart.
- Boyfriend's mother - fifth house love relationship (fourth house from the fifth house).
- Girlfriend's father - fifth house love relationship (fourth house from the fifth house).
- Father's second sibling in a female's chart.
- Mother's second sibling in a male's chart.
- Brothers and sisters of co-workers (third house from the sixth house).

Look to the eighth house for the above mentioned people when dealing with the affairs of one of them. Use the native's eighth house as the other's first house and read the remainder of them accordingly (native's ninth house is the other's second house, etc.). For each house note all natal and transiting planets, aspects made to them and the ruler of each house. The effects, in many cases, are experienced by the individuals listed above.

Native's Ninth House Is Another's Second House
The second house governs personal finances, moveable possessions, negotiable assets, profit and loss, personal wealth and how money is spent or saved.

The ninth house (the second house from the eighth house) governs money gained or lost through insurance policies, social security, retirement and alimony; money and moveable possessions gained or lost through inheritance and property of the deceased.

Those in the insurance industry often have aspects linking the ruler of the ninth with the ruler of the eighth; money (ninth house) through selling of insurance (eighth house).

Native's Tenth House Is Another's Third House
The third house governs all forms of communication; letters, phone calls, telegrams, books, documents and contracts; individual mental attributes, and primary and secondary education; short trips and all forms of transportation such as busses, automobiles, bicycles, and motor cycles; accidents and minor changes; and brothers, sisters and neighbors.

The tenth house (third house from the eighth house) governs news, communication or the reading of an obituary concerning the demise of another; short trips and documents connected with matters of the dead or an inheritance; signing papers, contracts or documents concerning other people's money, such as

40

mortgages, loans, alimony, insurance, retirement funds and social security.

Native's Eleventh House Is Another's Fourth House
The fourth house governs the home, real estate and property; emotional security and home environment; parents, family members and individuals who reside in the individual's home; older people; the grave and affairs surrounding the latter part of life.

The eleventh house (fourth house from the eighth) governs the final outcome of inheritances, insurance, wills, mortgage payments and alimony.

Native's Twelfth House Is Another's Fifth House
The fifth house governs children in general, offspring, love relationships, courtship, pleasure and personal creativity; all places of amusement, theaters, entertainment, parties, schools, sporting events and participation in games and sports; and gambling, speculation and investments.

The twelfth house (seventh house from the sixth house) governs union or company contracts that may affect changes regarding health or working conditions of employees.

Native's First House Is Another's Sixth House
The sixth house governs health and well being; foods for maintaining health (vitamins and health foods); the food industry and those connected with it in selling, processing or restaurant work; working conditions, co-workers and household appliance repairmen; inferiors, farmers, small pets and tenants; the armed forces, police, Red Cross, Peace Corps and other such volunteer organizations; clothing in general and individuals who deal with it such as dry cleaners, seamstresses and tailors; and aunts and uncles.

The first house (sixth house from the eighth house) reveals the circumstances and manner in which details concerning insurance, internal revenue, taxes, inheritances, debts, death and the resources of the mate's earnings are handled.

Native's Second House Is Another's Seventh House

The seventh house governs dealings with the general public, open enemies, litigation, contracts, physicians, attorneys, counselors and all things of beauty; marriage and business partners, live-in relationships and sweethearts; and nieces, nephews and grandparents.

Native's Third House Is Another's Eighth House

The eighth house governs money belonging to others; the partner's earnings, legacies, wills, credit card debt, loans and alimony; income and property taxes; sexuality, changes, surgery and conditions surrounding the manner of death; and nightmares, unusual dreams and compelling forces.

Native's Fourth House Is Another's Ninth House

The ninth house governs public opinion, philosophy, publishing, advertising, prophetic dreams and visions; religious affiliations, long trips, legal matters, newspapers and other published material; news from a distance; higher education; the patronage of individuals of wealth and influence and those of different colors, races and backgrounds.

The fourth house (ninth house from the eighth house) governs lawsuits and legal activities as a result of unpaid debts, insurance, inheritance and property belonging to the deceased; alimony payments; long distance travels or news from a distance in connection with a death occurring at a faraway place; interruption of travel plans or higher education as a result of a death.

Native's Fifth House Is Another's Tenth House

The tenth house governs credit rating, reputation, rank in life, scandal, career, trade and profession; those with authority over the native, the boss, parent and anyone representing influence and power; past conditions; and sometimes the culmination of a long standing situation.

The fifth house (tenth house from the eighth house) governs public attention, publicity and scandal surrounding the manner of death; public attention, publicity and scandal concerning inheritance, insurance settlements, property belonging to the deceased, alimony and questionable money gained through the resources of others such as a payoff from or to a person of disreputable character.

Native's Sixth House Is Another's Eleventh House

The eleventh house governs affiliations with clubs and organizations, and group activities; friends, acquaintances and individual aspirations; and daughters-in-law, sons-in-law and step-children. The sixth house governs friends made or met through the settlement of insurance claims or while dealing with matters of the deceased.

Native's Seventh House Is Another's Twelfth House

The twelfth house governs hospitals, charitable institutions and all places of confinement such as jails and prisons; secret enemies, secret sorrows, hidden relationships and clandestine affairs; detective, investigative and behind the scenes activities; suicides, drugs, alcohol, limitations and restrictions; unforeseen forces, incidents and circumstances secret, weird and unusual fears; and aunts and uncles.

The seventh house (twelfth house from the eighth house) governs hidden sorrows, losses and secrets regarding the demise of another person; secrets, sorrows, losses, or deception connected with money and moveable possessions of the marriage or business partner; secret fears and worries regarding sexual matters, life hereafter and death; secret sorrows, losses, deception or confusion with wills, insurance policies, inheritance and alimony.

Ninth House

The ninth house deals with philosophy, public opinion, publishing, advertising, prophetic dreams, visions and intuition; those who deal with future trends such as merchandise buyers, bankers, investors, economic and financial advisors, and weather forecasters; religion, ministers, priests, nuns and missionaries; long trips, legal matters, newspapers, books and other published material, and news from a distance; college and adult education classes; instructors and educators; the patronage of individuals of wealth or influence; good luck and future growth or expansion; charities, welfare, community services and aid to dependent children; judges and courts of law; contact with individuals who live at a distance or with those of different social levels, races, colors or nationality; strangers who enter an individual's life and play an important role. The ninth house also governs these people:

- Second marriage partner.
- Mate's first sibling.
- Business partner's first sibling.
- Third child in a male's chart.
- Grandchildren.
- Fourth sibling.
- Friend of a friend (eleventh house from the eleventh house).
- Marriage partner of the first sibling.
- Parent of a co-worker (fourth house from the sixth house).

Look to the ninth house for the above mentioned people when dealing with the affairs of one of them. Use the native's ninth house as the other's first and read the remainder of the chart accordingly (native's tenth house is the other's second house, etc.). For each house note all natal and transiting planets, aspects made to them and the ruler of each house. The effects, in many cases, are experienced by the individuals listed above.

Native's Tenth House Is Another's Second House

The second house governs personal finances, moveable possessions, negotiable assets, profit and loss, personal wealth and how money is spent or saved.

The tenth house (second house from the ninth house) governs financial gain or loss through travel, higher education, publications and foreign products or individuals.

Native's Eleventh House Is Another's Third House

The third house governs all forms of communication; letters, phone calls, telegrams, books, documents and contracts; individual mental attributes, and primary and secondary education; short trips and all forms of transportation such as busses, automobiles, bicycles and motorcycles; accidents and minor changes; and brothers, sisters, and neighbors.

The eleventh house (third house from the ninth house) governs contracts and short trips regarding books, publications and other printed material.

Native's Twelfth House Is Another's Fourth House

The fourth house governs the home, real estate and property; emotional security and home environment; parents, family members and individuals who reside in the native's home from time to time; older people; and the grave and affairs surrounding the latter part of life.

The twelfth house (fourth house from the ninth house) governs all motel and hotel stays during long distance travels and living conditions and residences when visiting foreign countries; the condition and saleability of any property, land or real estate the individual owns in a foreign country or different state; and living conditions and residences while attending college in another state.

Native's First House Is Another's Fifth House
The fifth house governs children in general, offspring, love relationships, courtship, pleasure and personal creativity; all places of amusement, theaters, entertainment, parties, schools, sporting events and participation in games and sports; gambling, speculation and investments.

The first house (fifth house from the ninth house) governs heart problems and love affairs of one's brother or sister-in-law.

Native's Second House Is Another's Sixth House
The sixth house governs health and well being; foods for maintaining health (vitamins and health foods); the food industry and those connected with it in selling, processing and restaurant work; working conditions, co-workers and household appliance repairmen; inferiors, farmers, small pets and tenants; the armed forces, police, Red Cross, Peace Corps and other such volunteer organizations; clothing in general and individuals who deal with it such as dry cleaners, seamstresses and tailors; and aunts and uncles.

The second house (sixth house from the ninth house) governs illness and physical comfort or discomfort while traveling;

health problems that may affect travel plans, publications or the individual's position as an instructor.

Native's Third House Is Another's Seventh House

The seventh house governs dealings with the general public, open enemies, litigation, contracts, physicians, attorneys, counselors and all things of beauty; marriage and business partners, live-in relationships and sweethearts; and nieces, nephews and grandparents.

The third house (seventh house from the ninth house) governs open enemies as they relate to published material offered by the individual; open enemies connected with matters of higher education or future plans.

Native's Fourth House Is Another's Eighth House

The eighth house governs money belonging to others; the partner's earnings, legacies, wills, credit card debt, loans and alimony; income and property taxes; sexuality, changes, surgery and conditions surrounding the manner of death; and nightmares, unusual dreams and compelling forces.

The fourth house (eighth house from the ninth house) governs inheritance and legacies from foreign countries or through those residing at a distance; changes affecting higher education or matters surrounding an activity in a foreign country.

Native's Fifth House Is Another's Ninth House

The ninth house governs public opinions, philosophy, publishing, advertising, prophetic dreams and visions; religious affiliations, long trips, legal matters, newspapers and other published material; news from a distance; higher education; the patronage of individuals of wealth and influence; and those of different colors, races and backgrounds.

The fifth house (ninth house from the ninth house) governs travel to promote published material, books, higher education and for organizations affiliated with religion.

Native's Sixth House Is Another's Tenth House

The tenth house governs credit rating, reputation, rank in life, scandal, career, trade and profession; those with authority over the individual, the boss, parent and anyone representing influence and power; past conditions; and sometimes the culmination of a long standing situation.

The sixth house (tenth house from the ninth house) governs public notice, publicity and scandal concerning lawsuits, publications or affiliations with ministers, priests and foreigners; public notice, publicity and scandal regarding the individual's role as an instructor in college or other fields of higher education.

Native's Seventh House Is Another's Eleventh House

The eleventh house governs affiliations with clubs and organizations, and group activities; friends, acquaintances and individual aspirations; and daughters-in-law, sons-in-law and step-children.

The seventh house (eleventh house from the ninth house) governs friendships made through college, foreign or long distance travel and religious organizations.

Native's Eighth House Is Another's Twelfth House

The twelfth house governs hospitals, charitable institutions and all places of confinement such as jails and prisons; secret enemies, secret sorrows, hidden relationships and clandestine affairs; detective, investigative and behind the scenes activities; suicides, drugs, alcohol, limitations and restrictions; unforeseen forces, incidents and circumstances; secret, weird and unusual fears; and aunts and uncles.

The eighth house (twelfth house from the ninth house) governs secrets, sorrows, deception, confusion and hidden factors regarding foreigners, lawsuits, legal matters, publications, religion, travel and higher education.

Tenth House

The tenth house governs ambition for success in the areas of status, wealth and public recognition; ability for handling responsibilities coupled with skillful maneuvering in overcoming obstacles; submission to those in authority while striving to achieve a position of authority; credit rating, reputation, scandal, rank in life, career, trade and profession; those with authority over the individual, the boss, superior and anyone representing influence and power; parent or an older, mature or serious individual; past conditions; sometimes the culmination of a long standing problem; administrators, presidents, mayors, councilmen and anyone paid by city, state or federal taxes. The tenth house also governs these people:

- Parents, step-parents and parents-in-law (female parent in a woman's chart, male parent in a male's chart).
- Fourth child in a female's chart.
- Boss or employer.
- Father's third sibling in a female's chart.
- Mother's third sibling in a male's chart.
- Cousins (first child of the sixth house aunt or uncle).
- Husband or wife of the first child in a woman's chart.
- Child of a co-worker (fifth house from the sixth house).

Look to the tenth house for the above mentioned people when dealing with the affairs of one of them. Use the native's tenth house as the other's first and read the remainder of the chart accordingly (Native's eleventh house is the other's second house). For each house note all natal or transiting planets, aspects made to them and the ruler of each house. The effects, in many cases, are experienced by the individuals listed above.

Native's Eleventh House Is Another's Second House.

The second house governs personal finances, moveable possessions, negotiable assets, profit and loss, personal wealth and how money is spent and saved.

The eleventh house (second house from the tenth house) governs money, moveable possessions and income obtained through the business or profession.

Native's Twelfth House Is Another's Third House

The third house governs all forms of communication; letters, phone calls, telegrams, books, documents and contracts; individual mental attributes, and primary and secondary education; short trips and all forms of transportation such as busses, automobiles, bicycles and motorcycles; accidents and minor changes; and brothers, sisters and neighbors.

The twelfth house (third house from the tenth) governs contracts and short trips in connection with the business or profession.

Native's First House Is Another's Fourth House

The fourth house governs the home, real estate and property; emotional security and home environment; parents, family members and individuals who reside in the individual's home from time to time; older people; the grave and the affairs surrounding the latter part of life.

The first house (fourth house from the tenth house) governs the final outcome or end of the matter concerning a boss's decision or career change.

Native's Second House Is Another's Fifth House

The fifth house governs children in general, offspring, love relationships, courtship, pleasure and personal creativity; all places of amusements, theaters, entertainment, parties, schools, sporting events and participation in games and sports; and gambling, speculation and investments.

The second house (fifth house from the tenth house) governs the general heart condition of a boss or parent.

Native's Third House Is Another's Sixth House

The sixth house governs health and well being; foods for maintaining health (vitamins and health foods); the food industry and those connected with it in selling, processing and restaurant work; working conditions, co-workers and household appliance repairmen; inferiors, farmers, small pets and tenants; the armed forces, police, Red Cross, Peace Corps and other such volunteer organizations; clothing in general and individuals who deal with it such as dry cleaners, seamstress and tailors; and aunts and uncles.

The third house (sixth house from the tenth house) governs volunteer services and work performed for the government, city officials and political parties, and volunteer work for a boss that is separate from company duties such as helping to paint his house.

Native's Fourth House Is Another's Seventh House

The seventh house governs dealings with the general public, open enemies, litigation, contracts, physicians, attorneys, coun-

selors and all things of beauty; marriage and business partners, live-in relationships and sweethearts; and nieces, nephews and grandparents.

The fourth house (seventh house from the tenth house) governs litigation resulting from damage to the credit rating, reputation and status.

Native's Fifth House Is Another's Eighth House
The eighth house governs money belonging to others; the partner's earnings, legacies, wills, debts to stores, loans and alimony; income and property taxes; sexuality, changes, surgery and conditions surrounding the manner of death; nightmares, unusual dreams and compelling forces.

The fifth house (eighth house from the tenth house) governs death of a career due to the public's likes or dislikes, such as the loss of a city, state or federal election, or through changes taking place within the company.

Native's Sixth House Is Another's Ninth House
The ninth house governs public opinion, philosophy, publishing, advertising, prophetic dreams and visions; religious affiliations, long trips, legal matters, newspapers and other published material; news from a distance; higher education; the patronage of individuals of wealth and influence and those of different colors, races and backgrounds.

The sixth house (ninth house from the tenth house) governs higher education as it enhances career or professional potential; travel that is work related or undertaken to promote professional standing; and lawsuits against the company through age, sex or racial discrimination.

Native's Seventh House Is Another's Tenth House

The tenth house governs credit rating, reputation, rank in life, scandal, career, trade and profession; those with authority over the native, the boss, parent and anyone representing influence and power; past conditions; and sometimes the culmination of a long standing situation.

The seventh house (tenth house from the tenth house) governs public standing, scandal, rank, reputation, and business or professional credit rating. This house often determines if and when the individual's company or employer is going to file bankruptcy or lose its good credit rating. If the boss is having problems with his boss, this house will help determine the problem.

Native's Eighth House Is Another's Eleventh House

The eleventh house governs affiliations with clubs and organizations, and group activities; friends, acquaintances and the individual's aspirations; and daughters-in-law, sons-in-law and step-children.

The eighth house (eleventh house from the tenth house) governs aspirations connected with profession or career and friends made through business deals.

Native's Ninth House Is Another's Twelfth House

The twelfth house governs hospitals, charitable institutions and all places of confinement such as jails and prisons; secret enemies, secret sorrows, hidden relationships and clandestine affairs; detective, investigative and behind the scenes activities; suicides, drugs, alcohol, limitations and restrictions; unforeseen forces, incidents and circumstances; secret, weird and unusual fears; and aunts and uncles.

The ninth house (twelfth house from the tenth house) governs secrets, sorrows, limitations, and losses through business and profession; secrets concerning credit rating, public image and reputation; and confusion or deceptive or chaotic conditions going on behind the work scene and generated by one's boss or other figure of authority.

Eleventh House

The eleventh house deals with new, progressive, unconventional and unexpected events and circumstances; affairs concerned with astrology, friends, acquaintances, clubs and organizations and individual aspirations; and activities dealing with inventions, radio, TV, electricity, automobiles, modern mechanical devices and engineers. The eleventh house also governs these people:

- Friends.
- Step-children and adopted children.
- Daughters-in-law and sons-in-law (generally the spouse of the first child in a male's chart).
- Fourth child in a male's chart.
- Fifth sibling.
- Marriage partner of the second sibling.
- First mate or business partner's second sibling.
- Love relationships of nieces and nephews (children of the individual's sibling).
- Love relationships of nieces and nephews (children of the individual's sibling).
- Love relationship of the first mate or business partner.

Look to the eleventh house for the above mentioned people when dealing with the affairs of one of them. Use the native's eleventh house as the other's first house and read the remainder of the chart accordingly (native's twelfth is the other's second house, etc.). For each house note all natal and transiting planets, aspects made to them and the ruler of each house. The effects, in many cases, are experienced by the individuals listed above.

Native's Twelfth House Is Another's Second House
The second house governs personal finances, moveable possessions, negotiable assets, profit and loss, personal wealth and how money is spent and saved.

The twelfth house (second house from the eleventh house) governs money, moveable possessions and financial benefit or loss connected with clubs and organizations.

Native's First House Is Another's Third House
The third house governs all forms of communication; letters, phone calls, telegrams, books, documents and contracts; individual mental attributes, and primary and second education; short trips and all forms of transportation such as busses, automobiles, bicycles and motorcycles; accidents and minor changes; and brothers, sisters and neighbors.

The first house (third house from the eleventh house) governs all correspondence, communication, news and short trips related to clubs and organizations.

Native's Second House Is Another's Fourth House
The fourth house governs the home, real estate and property; emotional security and home environment; parents, family members and individuals who reside in the home from time to time; older people; the grave and the affairs surrounding the latter part of life.

The second house (fourth house from the eleventh house) governs the final outcome concerning clubs and organizations; and property belonging to clubs and organizations.

Native's Third House Is Another's Fifth House

The fifth house governs children in general, offspring, love relationships, courtship, pleasure and personal creativity; all places of amusement, theaters, entertainment, parties, schools, sporting events and participation in games and sports; and gambling, speculation and investments.

The third house (fifth house from the eleventh house) governs the kind of entertainment sought by clubs and organization to which the individual belongs; check transits and aspects to the third house.

Native's Fourth House Is Another's Sixth House

The sixth house governs health and well being; foods for maintaining health (vitamins and health foods); the food industry and those connected with it in selling, processing and restaurant work; working conditions, co-workers and household appliance repairmen; inferiors, farmers, small pets and tenants; the armed forces, police, Red Cross, Peace Corps and other such volunteer organizations; clothing in general and individuals who deal with it such as dry cleaners, seamstresses and tailors; and aunts and uncles.

The fourth house (sixth house from the eleventh house) governs volunteer services the individual performs for clubs and organizations.

Native's Fifth House Is Another's Seventh House

The seventh house governs dealings with the general public, open enemies, litigation, contracts, physicians, attorneys, coun-

selors and all things of beauty; marriages and business partners, live-in relationships and sweethearts; and nieces, nephews and grandparents.

The fifth house (seventh house from the eleventh house) governs open enemies of one's club or organization.

Native's Sixth House Is Another's Eighth House

The eighth house governs money belonging to others; the partner's earnings, legacies, wills, credit card debts, loans and alimony; income and property taxes; sexuality, changes, surgery and conditions surrounding the manner of death; nightmares, unusual dreams and compelling forces.

The sixth house (eighth house from the eleventh house) governs debts and mutual financial holdings of one's club or organization.

Native's Seventh House Is Another's Ninth House

The ninth house governs public opinion, philosophy, publishing, advertising, prophetic dreams and visions; religious affiliations, long trips, legal matters, newspapers and other published material; news from a distance; higher education; the patronage of individuals of wealth and influence; and those of different colors, races and backgrounds.

The seventh house (ninth house from the eleventh house) governs all legal matters, distant travels and correspondences connected with clubs and organizations; news, correspondence, visits from or to friends residing at a distance.

Native's Eighth House Is Another's Tenth House

The tenth house governs credit rating, reputation, rank in life, scandal, career, trade and profession; those with authority over the native, the boss, parent and anyone representing influence and power; past conditions; and sometimes the culmination of a long standing situation.

The eighth house (tenth house from the eleventh house) governs public standing, recognition and the reputation of clubs and organizations to which the individual belongs; public notice, acclaim and recognition for work and efforts performed for a fraternal organization; prominent and prestigious positions for clubs and organization.

Native's Ninth House Is Another's Eleventh House

The eleventh house governs affiliations with clubs and organizations, and group activities; friends, acquaintances and individual aspirations; and daughters-in-law, sons-in-law and step-children.

The ninth house (eleventh house from the eleventh house) governs making new friends or acquaintances at seminars or conferences who are from foreign countries or states other than the one in which the native resides.

Native's Tenth House Is Another's Twelfth House

The twelfth house governs hospitals, charitable institutions and all places of confinement such as jails and prisons; secret enemies, secret sorrows, hidden relationships and clandestine affairs; detective, investigative and behind the scenes activities; suicides, drugs, alcohol, limitations and restrictions; unforeseen forces, incidents and circumstances; secret, weird, and unusual fears; and aunts and uncles.

The tenth house (twelfth house from the eleventh house) governs secrets, sorrows, limitation, deception and confusion of or through friends; secrets, deception and elements of confusion surrounding clubs and organizations.

62

T_{welfth} H_{ouse}

The twelfth house deals with impressions surroundings make on the individual with a tendency to pick up vibrations in the immediate environment, whether good or bad. In the positive sense, this is the house of lofty, idealistic and refined ideas. It also deals with the promotion of others whom the individual feels are deserving. Negatively, the individual may try to withdraw from reality; therefore, it is also the house of escapism. Various individuals seek different means of escapism; some through abuse of drugs or alcohol, and others through day dreaming or extended sleep. This also is the house of psychism and witchcraft, and governs how the individual compassionately and sympathetically responds to others.

The affairs of this house are concerned with hospitals, charitable institutions and all places of confinement such as jails and prisons; secret enemies, secret sorrows, hidden relationships, clandestine affairs, detective, investigative and behind the scenes activities; suicides, addictive drugs, limitations and restrictions; unforeseen forces, incidents and circumstances; secret, weird and unusual fears. The twelfth house also governs these people:

- Aunts and uncles on the father's side in a male's chart and the mother's side in a female chart.

- Secret enemy.
- Fifth child in a female's chart.
- Co-worker's marriage partner (seventh house from the sixth house).
- Boss or those in authority over the first sibling (tenth house from the third house).
- Mate's co-worker (sixth house from the seventh house).

Look to the twelfth house for the above mentioned people when dealing with the affairs of one of them. Use the native's twelfth house as the other's first and read the remainder of the chart accordingly (native's first house is the other's second, etc.). For each house note all natal and transiting planets, aspects made to them and the ruler of each house. The effects, in many cases, are experienced by the individuals listed above.

Native's First House Is Another's Second House

The second house governing personal finances, moveable possessions, negotiable assets, profit and loss, personal wealth and how money is spent and saved.

The first house (second house from the twelfth house) governs financial gain or loss of one's aunt or uncle and secret enemies.

Native's Second House Is Another's Third House

The third house governs all forms of communication; letters, phone calls, telegrams, books, documents and contracts; individual mental attributes, and primary and secondary education; short trips and all forms of transportation such as busses, automobiles, bicycles and motorcycles; accidents and minor changes; and brothers, sisters and neighbors.

The second house (third house from the twelfth) governs short trips and communication in connection with psychiatric treatments, hospitalization and other places of confinement; letters, phone calls and secret, short trips for clandestine activities.

Native's Third House is Another's Fourth House

The fourth house governs the home, real estate and property; emotional security and home environment; parents, family members and individuals who reside in the home from time to time; older people; and the grave and the affairs surrounding the latter part of life.

The third house (fourth house from the twelfth house) governs the home condition and property of clandestine lovers and aunts and uncles.

Native's Fourth House Is Another's Fifth House

The fifth house governs children in general, offspring, love relationships, courtship, pleasure and personal creativity; all places of amusement, theaters, entertainment, parties, schools, sporting events and participation in games and sports; and gambling, speculation and investments.

The fourth house (fifth house from the twelfth house) governs the heart condition of aunts and uncles and their romantic affairs.

Native's Fifth House Is Another's Sixth House

The sixth house governs health and well being; foods for maintaining health (vitamins and health foods); the food industry and those connected with it in selling, processing and restaurant work; working conditions, co-workers and household appliance repairmen; inferiors, farmers, small pets and tenants; the armed forces, police, Red Cross, Peace Corps and other such volunteer organizations; clothing in general and individuals who deal with it such as dry cleaners, seamstresses and tailors; and aunts and uncles.

The fifth house (sixth house from the twelfth) governs health problems that are caused by stressful environmental conditions such as excessive noise, confusion and repeated arguments; and health conditions that can be improved or impaired through the use of certain drugs and medications.

Native's Sixth House Is Another's Seventh House
The seventh house governs the general public, open enemies, litigation, contracts, physicians, attorneys, counselors and all things of beauty; marriage and business partners, live-in relationships and sweethearts; and nieces, nephews and grandparents.

The sixth house (seventh house from the twelfth) governs behind-the-scenes partnerships that remain secret.

Native's Seventh House Is Another's Eighth House
The eighth house governs money belonging to others; the partner's earnings, legacies, wills, credit card debt, loans and alimony; income and property taxes; sexuality, changes, surgery and conditions surrounding the manner of death; and nightmares, unusual dreams and compelling forces.

The seventh house (eighth house from the twelfth house) governs the death, change of attitude toward or loss of clandestine affairs; and death or surgery of aunts and uncles.

Native's Eighth House Is Another's Ninth House
The ninth house governs public opinion, philosophy, publishing, advertising, prophetic dreams and visions; religious af-

filiations, long trips, legal matters, newspapers and other published material; news from a distance; higher education; the patronage of individuals of wealth and influence; and those of different colors, races and backgrounds.

The eighth house (ninth house from the twelfth house) governs lawsuits involving hospitals, institutions and clandestine relationships; long distance trips taken in secrecy or because of a clandestine relationship; personal items that are stolen (twelfth house thief) while visiting a foreign country or while traveling; higher education and distant travels to increase knowledge in the fields of astrology, the occult, psychic phenomena and meditation.

Native's Ninth House Is Another's Tenth House
The ninth house governs credit rating, reputation, rank in life, scandal, career, trade and profession; those with authority over the individual, the boss, parent and anyone representing influence and power; past conditions; and sometimes the culmination of a long standing situation.

The ninth house (tenth house from the twelfth house) governs publicity or scandal surrounding imprisonment, confinement and institutional stays; and career and reputation of one's aunt or uncle and one's clandestine affair.

Native's Tenth House Is Another's Eleventh House
The eleventh house governs affiliations with clubs and organizations, and group activities; friends, acquaintances and individual aspirations; and daughters-in-law, sons-in-law and step-children.

The tenth house (eleventh house from the twelfth house) governs friends and club affiliations of one's aunt, uncle or clandestine lover.

Native's Eleventh House Is Another's Twelfth House

The twelfth house governs hospitals, charitable institutions and all places of confinement such as jails and prisons; secret enemies, secret sorrows, hidden relationships and clandestine affairs; detective, investigative and behind the scenes activities; suicides, drugs, alcohol, limitations and restrictions; unforeseen forces, incidents and circumstances; secret, weird and unusual fears; and aunts and uncles.

Sample Charts

When Bill Clinton won the presidential election in November, 1992, I decided to try my hand at projecting an important event that appeared imminent for March, 1993.

I added an extra page to one of my correspondence courses at that time to cover the event for the upcoming month of March and in December, 1992 we did President Clinton's chart at Valley Forge High School in an adult continuing education astrology class.

It was my intention to prove to the students (correspondence and evening classes) that it is possible to project an event months ahead with proper knowledge and procedure.

It was the Solar and Lunar Eclipse of December that brought President Clinton's chart to my attention.

The Lunar Eclipse of December 9, 1992 was at 18 degrees Gemini conjunct Clinton's Uranus at 21 Gemini in his ninth house of in-laws and distant matters. Uranus rules his natal fifth house (eighth house - death - from the tenth house - parent). The Lunar Eclipse also made a semisquare aspect to his natal Saturn at two degrees Leo in his natal tenth house.

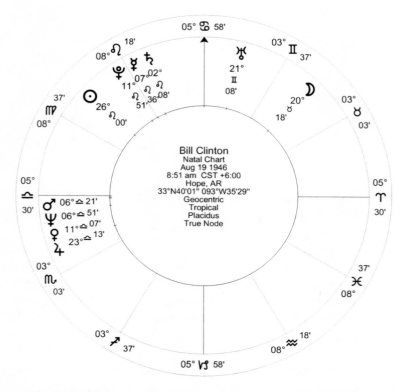

The Solar Eclipse of December 24, 1992 at 2 Capricorn made
an exact inconjunct to his natal Saturn at two degrees Leo in his
natal tenth house of parents.

When a planet in the natal tenth house is highlighted by an
eclipse (Solar Eclipse inconjunct natal Saturn) and the ruler of
the natal fifth house (eighth house from the tenth house) is also
highlighted by an eclipse (Lunar Eclipse conjunct natal Uranus,
ruler of the natal fifth house) we can assume that a parent may
be a source of concern in terms of surgery or loss.

When "both" Solar and Lunar Eclipses aspect natal planets it
usually foretells a major event and the usual procedure is to look

ahead for New and Full Moons that will fortify the event promised by the two previous eclipses.

The Full Moon of March 8, 1993 was at 17 Virgo 50 and it fell in President Clinton's twelfth house squaring his natal Uranus and the previous Lunar Eclipse of 18 Gemini.

Transiting Mercury on the day of the Lunar Eclipse was retrograding at 19 Pisces and the next day Mercury would be at 18 Pisces exactly squaring the Lunar Eclipse position. Mercury rules his ninth house of in-laws and distant matters, fortifying the Lunar Eclipse position in his ninth house.

Transiting Venus was positioned in his natal seventh house at 19 Aries 51, squaring transiting Neptune at 20 Capricorn in his natal fourth house. Transiting Venus turned retrograde a few days later at 20 Aries, exactly square transiting Neptune at 20 Capricorn.

Transiting Mars on the day of the Lunar Eclipse was at 11 Cancer in his natal tenth house, squaring his natal Venus at 11 Libra, which was conjunct transiting Jupiter retrograding at 11 Libra. Transiting mars rules his natal seventh house and transiting Jupiter rules his natal third house (ninth house from the seventh house). When two transits are in aspect with one another (Mars square Jupiter), the faster planet (Mars) provides the starting point and Jupiter indicates the consequences of the house Mars rules. In other words, something important would involve Clinton's wife (Mars rules the seventh house) and it would take place at a distance because Jupiter rules the third house (ninth house from the seventh house).

One last aspect has to be given serious consideration: transiting Saturn at 24 Aquarius in his natal fifth house (the

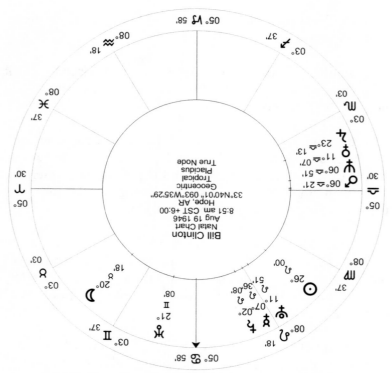

Bill Clinton's Chart in a Seventh House Position

house cusp ruler, Uranus, was highlighted by the Lunar Eclipse) would soon be squaring transiting Pluto in his natal second house.

Fifty percent of my evening class students projected that President Clinton would suffer a health problem (Full Moon in Virgo falling in his twelfth and sixth houses). However they forgot one important rule: when a transiting planet is positioned in a natal house (transiting Venus in his natal seventh house) and the ruler of the natal house cusp is also highlighted (transiting Mars ruler of the seventh house was in square aspect with Clinton's natal Venus and also transiting Jupiter in Libra in his first house), the focal point will be centered on the natal house (in this case the seventh house).

With the focal point leading to the seventh house, we turn President Clinton's chart around to place the seventh house in a first house position (for ease in reading the chart). From there we will determine the effect that the New and Full Moons and transits of March 1993 had on his wife Hillary Clinton.

The Lunar Eclipse of December 9, 1992 at 18 degrees Gemini fell in Hillary Clinton's third house of communication and was conjunct natal Uranus in the natal third house. She was to hear some unexpected and disturbing news concerning an older member of the family as the Lunar Eclipse was semi-square natal Saturn at 2 Leo positioned in her fourth house.

The Solar Eclipse of December 24, 1992 at 2 Capricorn took place in her ninth house (indicating someone who lives in a distant city or an in-law) and inconjuncts natal Saturn in her fourth house (her parent at a distance).

Someone would be in the hospital with transiting retrograde Mercury at 19 Pisces in the twelfth house squaring the Lunar Eclipse on the next day (March 9, 1993) from 18 degrees Pisces. Transiting Mercury rules the third house containing both the Lunar Eclipse and natal Uranus.

Transiting Venus was in her first house at 19 Aries 50, soon to turn retrograde at 20 Aries and exactly square transiting Neptune at 20 Capricorn in her natal tenth house.

With transiting Neptune ruling the twelfth house and transiting Mercury therein in Pisces, this provided additional confirmation that a family member would soon enter the hospital.

Hillary's ruling planet Mars (Aries on the Ascendant) was at 11 Cancer in her natal fourth house of parent squaring natal Venus at 11 Libra and transiting retrograde Jupiter at 12 Libra. Transiting Jupiter conjunct Venus, ruler of her seventh house, indicated that her husband would be taking a trip with her (transiting Mars ruler of her first house was squaring natal Venus, ruler of her seventh house of marriage partner). The square from transiting Mars to transiting Jupiter conjunct natal Venus provided the additional insight that travel to a distant city would be due to difficult circumstances (squares) concerning a family member of Hillary's.

Another confirmation of a parental demise was transiting Saturn at 25 Aquarius in her eleventh house (eighth house from the fourth house) square transiting Pluto in her natal eighth house.

Hillary's father suffered a stroke and she remained by his bedside for the nine days that he remained hospitalized before passing away shortly after the New Moon at 2 Aries, which squared the previous Solar Eclipse of December 24, 1992 at 2 Capricorn. Apparently recovery was not imminent as the New Moon at two degrees Aries exactly trined natal Saturn at two degrees Leo, indicating that the trine would be a blessed ending to his suffering.

In December 1992 I had no knowledge of Hillary Clinton's family background. I could only project to my students that Hillary Clinton would be gravely concerned over the health of an older family member who lived in a distant city. In March 1993, Hillary was in Washington, DC at the time of her father's death which occurred in a distant city.

Printed in the United States
121356LV00002B/1-48/P

9 780866 903639